DISCOVER DOGS WITH THE AMERICAN CANINE ASSOCIATION

I LIKE COCKER SPANIELS!

Linda Bozzo

It is the mission of the American Canine Association (ACA) to provide registered dog owners with the educational support needed for raising, training, showing, and breeding the healthiest pets expected by responsible pet owners throughout the world. Through our activities and services, we encourage and support the dog world in order to promote best-known husbandry standards as well as to ensure that the voice and needs of our customers are quickly and properly addressed.

Our continued support, commitment, and direction are guided by our customers, including veterinary, legal, and legislative advisors. ACA aims to provide the most efficient, cooperative, and courteous service to our customers and strives to set the standard for education and problem solving for all who depend on our services.

For more information, please visit www.acacanines.com, email customerservice@acadogs.com, phone 1-800-651-8332, or write to the American Canine Association at PO Box 121107, Clermont, FL 34712.

Published in 2018 by Enslow Publishing, LLC.
101 W. 23rd Street, Suite 240, New York, NY 10011

Library of Congress Cataloging-in-Publication Data

Names: Bozzo, Linda, author.
Title: I like cocker spaniels! / Linda Bozzo.
Description: New York, NY : Enslow Publishing, 2018. | Series: Discover dogs with the American Canine Association | Includes bibliographical references and index. | Audience: Grades K to 3.
Identifiers: LCCN 2017011342| ISBN 9780766091337 (library bound) | ISBN 9780766091313 (pbk.) | ISBN 9780766091320 (6 pack)
Subjects: LCSH: Cocker spaniels—Juvenile literature.
Classification: LCC SF429.C55 B69 2017 | DDC 636.752/4—dc23
LC record available at https://lccn.loc.gov/2017011342

Printed in China

To Our Readers: We have done our best to make sure all websites in this book were active and appropriate when we went to press. However, the author and the publisher have no control over and assume no liability for the material available on those websites or on any websites they may link to. Any comments or suggestions can be sent by email to customerservice@enslow.com.

Photo Credits: Cover, p. 1 cynoclub/Shutterstock.com; p. 3 (left) WilleeCole Photography/Shutterstock.com; p. 3 (right) rebeccaashworth/Shutterstock .com; p. 5 Auscape/Universal Images Group/Getty Images; p. 6 otsphoto/Shutterstock.com; p. 9 Andrea Izzotti/Shutterstock.com; p. 10 Life In Pixels/ Shutterstock.com; p. 13 (puppy) © vladacanon/iStock/Thinkstock; p. 13 (collar) © graphicphoto/iStock/Thinkstock, (bed) Luisa Leal Photography/ Shutterstock.com, (brush) In-Finity/Shutterstock.com, (food and water bowls) exopixel/Shutterstock.com, (leash, toys) © iStockphoto.com/Liliboas; p. 14 © toxawww/iStock/Thinkstock; p. 17 © DevidDO/iStock/Thinkstock; p. 18 © iStockphoto.com/belchonock; p. 19 © Jupiterimages/Stockbyte/Thinkstock; p. 21 Africa Studio/Shutterstock.com.

Enslow Publishing
101 W. 23rd Street
Suite 240
New York, NY 10011
USA
enslow.com

CONTENTS

IS A COCKER SPANIEL RIGHT FOR YOU?

Cocker spaniels make great family pets. They can live anywhere as long as they can get their exercise. Most cocker spaniels are friendly with other pets.

Compared to other sporting dogs, the cocker spaniel is small in size.

A DOG OR A PUPPY?

Cocker spaniel puppies are always ready to learn. But training takes time. If you do not have time to train a puppy, you may want an older cocker spaniel instead.

Training cocker spaniels should be fun and playful.

LOVING YOUR COCKER SPANIEL

Love your cocker spaniel by teaching him tricks. Running and playing with your cocker spaniel will make him a happy dog.

Most cocker spaniels enjoy swimming.

EXERCISE

Cocker spaniels enjoy walks on a **leash**. This playful pooch will want to play games, like **fetch**.

Cocker spaniels were bred to be hunting dogs.

FEEDING YOUR COCKER SPANIEL

Cocker spaniels can be fed wet or dry dog food. Ask a **veterinarian (vet)**, a doctor for animals, which food is best for your dog and how much to feed her.

Give your cocker spaniel fresh, clean water every day.

Remember to keep your dog's food and water dishes clean. Dirty dishes can make a dog sick.

Do not feed your dog people food. It can make her sick.

Your new dog will need:

a collar with a tag

a bed

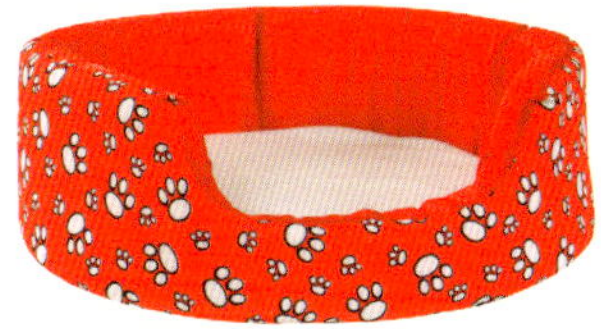

a brush

food and water dishes

a leash

toys

Cocker spaniels need professional grooming several times a year.

GROOMING

Cocker spaniels have lots of hair and **shed**. This means their hair falls out. Your cocker spaniel will need to be brushed every day and bathed when needed. Use a gentle soap made just for dogs.

A cocker spaniel's nails will need to be clipped. A vet or **groomer** can show you how. Your dog's ears should be cleaned, and his teeth should be brushed by an adult.

WHAT YOU SHOULD KNOW

Grooming a cocker spaniel takes lots of time. This breed is very friendly, so they don't make good watch dogs. Cocker spaniels may bark if left alone too long.

You will need to take your new dog to the vet for a checkup. He will need shots, called vaccinations, and yearly checkups to keep him healthy. If you think your dog may be sick or hurt, call your vet.

A GOOD FRIEND

Cocker spaniels are not only beautiful to look at, they also make good friends. These loving, gentle dogs can live as long as 10 to 15 years.

The word "spaniel" means "Spanish dog."

NOTE TO PARENTS

It is important to consider having your dog spayed or neutered when the dog is young. Spaying and neutering are operations that prevent unwanted puppies and can help improve the overall health of your dog.

It is also a good idea to microchip your dog, in case he or she gets lost. A vet will implant a microchip under the skin containing an identification number that can be scanned at a vet's office or animal shelter. The microchip registry is contacted, and the company uses the ID number to look up your information from a database.

Some towns require licenses for dogs, so be sure to check with your town clerk.

For more information, speak with a vet.

There are many dogs, young and old, waiting to be adopted from animal shelters and rescue groups.

Words to Know

fetch To go after a toy and bring it back.

groomer A person who bathes and brushes dogs.

leash A chain or strap that attaches to the dog's collar.

shed When dog hair falls out so new hair can grow.

vaccinations Shots that dogs need to stay healthy.

veterinarian (vet) A doctor for animals.

Read About Dogs

Books

Carney, Elizabeth. *Woof! 100 Fun Facts About Dogs.* Washington, DC: National Geographic Children's Books, 2017.

Gray, Susan H. *Cocker Spaniels.* New York, NY: AV2 Weigl, 2017.

Sommer, Nathan. *Cocker Spaniels.* Minneapolis, MN: Bellweather Media, Inc., 2018.

Websites

American Canine Association Inc., Kids Corner
www.acakids.com
Visit the official website of the American Canine Association.

National Geographic for Kids, Pet Central
kids.nationalgeographic.com/explore/pet-central/
Learn more about dogs and other pets at the official site of the National Geographic Society for Kids.

INDEX